D0908846

THE SECRET WORLD OF

Whales

THE SECRET WORLD OF

Whales

Theresa Greenaway

RAINTREE
Steck-Vaughn
PUBLISHERS

A Harcourt Company

Austin   New York
www.raintreesteckvaughn.com

Published by Raintree Steck-Vaughn Publishers, an imprint of Steck-Vaughn Company

Acknowledgments
Project Editors: Sean Dolan and Kathryn Walker
Consultant: David Larwa
Illustrated by Colin Newman
Designed by Ian Winton

Planned and produced by Discovery Books

Library of Congress Cataloging-in-Publication Data

Greenaway, Theresa, 1947-
Whales / Theresa Greenaway.
p. cm. -- (The secret world of)
Includes bibliographical references (p.).
ISBN 0-7398-3508-4
1. Whales--Juvenile literature. [1. Whales.] I. Title.

QL737.C4 G737 2001
599.5--dc21

00-062828

Printed and bound in the United States
1 2 3 4 5 6 7 8 9 LB 05 04 03 02 01

Contents

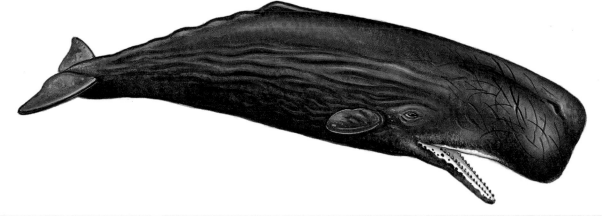

CHAPTER 1
Back to the Sea

Just like humans, whales are warm-blooded, air-breathing mammals that feed their young from their own body. Millions of years ago, the ancestors of whales had four limbs and walked on land. They searched for food at the edges of rivers and seas. Gradually they spent more and more time in the water, eventually becoming specialized for a fully aquatic life. Whales now live, feed, mate, and give birth in water, although they still have to come to the surface to breathe.

Dorsal fin
The dorsal fin of a humpback is small compared to its large body. Some whales have no dorsal fin at all.

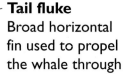

Tail fluke
Broad horizontal fin used to propel the whale through the water.

The blue whale is the largest animal that has ever lived. The maximum known length for a male is 102 feet (31 m), and for a female is 108 feet (33 m).

An average-sized blue whale weighs 80-120 tons (81-122 metric tons), but a really big blue whale can weigh as much as 150 tons (152 metric tons).

Right and bowhead whales weigh on average from 30 to 80 tons (30-81 metric tons).

The sperm whale is the largest toothed whale.

The smallest whale is the Gulf of California harbor porpoise, which is also known as the Vaquita or Cochito. Its maximum length is 4 feet 6 inches (1.4 m).

The bowhead whale has the longest plates of baleen.

There are about 80 different kinds, or species, of whales. They are all carnivores, eating a variety of other sea animals. Whales are divided into two groups, those with teeth and those that have horny plates, called baleen, instead of teeth. There are 10 kinds of baleen whales, the group that includes most of the really large whales, such as the blue, bowhead, and humpback whale. All the other kinds of whales, including dolphins and porpoises, are toothed whales. Dolphins and porpoises are often defined as small whales, although some kinds, such as the orca (killer whale) and pilot whale, are quite large.

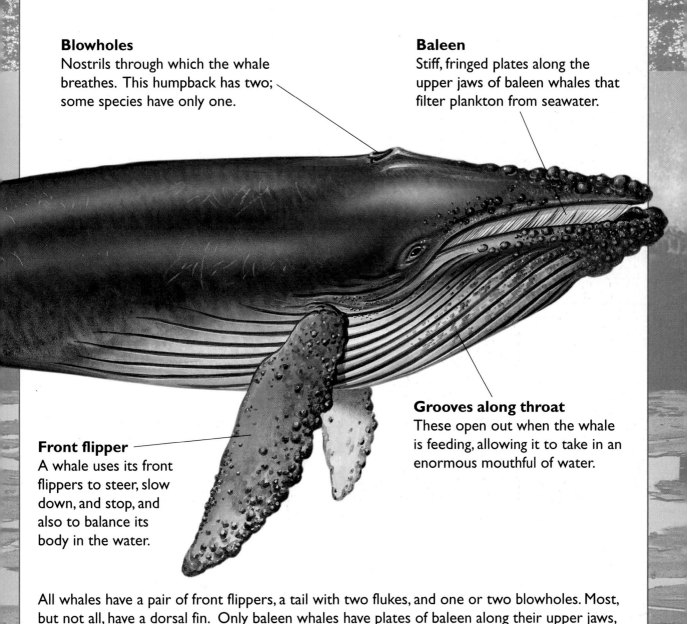

Blowholes
Nostrils through which the whale breathes. This humpback has two; some species have only one.

Baleen
Stiff, fringed plates along the upper jaws of baleen whales that filter plankton from seawater.

Front flipper
A whale uses its front flippers to steer, slow down, and stop, and also to balance its body in the water.

Grooves along throat
These open out when the whale is feeding, allowing it to take in an enormous mouthful of water.

All whales have a pair of front flippers, a tail with two flukes, and one or two blowholes. Most, but not all, have a dorsal fin. Only baleen whales have plates of baleen along their upper jaws, and only the rorquals have long grooves along the throat, as seen in this humpback whale.

The right whale filters plankton from seawater through its baleen. The lump on its head is a patch of rough skin, to which barnacles often cling.

Whales have a streamlined, fishlike shape. Instead of forelimbs they have broad flippers, and they have no hind limbs. Most species have a dorsal fin on their backs. Others, such as the sperm whale and the humpback, have a ridge of lumps along their backs, but the right and bowhead whales have neither. The tail consists of a pair of broad, horizontal fins called flukes.

A whale's head is different from a land mammal's head. Whales do not have large outer ears. Instead, a whale's ears are just a tiny hole on each side of its head. A whale has small eyes, and most can see underwater and in air. Whales breathe in air through one or two nostrils that are on the top of its head. These nostrils are called blowholes.

BALEEN WHALES

Baleen whales do not have any teeth. Instead, they have plates of a horny substance, keratin, that hang side by side along the upper jaws. These plates are called baleen. Each plate has a fringe of fibers down one side. Like our fingernails and hair, which are also made of keratin, baleen plates grow continuously, so that as they wear away, they are replaced. The baleen is used during feeding to strain small sea animals from seawater.

TOOTHED WHALES

All toothed whales have teeth, but the number of teeth varies by species. Dolphins have many teeth on both the upper and lower jaws. The long-snouted spinner dolphin has the most of all, sometimes as many as 260! Some types of beaked whales, such as the narwhal, have just two teeth. Only one of the narwhal's teeth is usually seen. This grows into a very long tusk, but the other tooth stays small and hidden in the whale's mouth.

Like those of this orca (or killer whale), most whales' teeth are cone-shaped. These sharply pointed teeth are good at gripping wriggling or slippery prey but cannot chew or grind food.

The dappled coloring of this spotted dolphin makes it harder for predators to see against the light and shadow created by sunlight on the water.

are dappled with spots. The common dolphin is the most colorful whale, with patches of yellow as well as black, white, and gray.

Individual whales are easy to identify, even out at sea. The right whale has patches of thickened skin on its head, which differ slightly from whale to whale. Each humpback whale has its own pattern of white markings on the underside of its tail flukes. These are clearly visible when the whale lifts its tail above the surface of the sea.

COLOR AND PATTERN

Whales have smooth, almost hairless skin. Most whales are gray in color, but the beluga is white and the bowhead whale is completely black except for a white chin. Many dolphins, including the orca, are patterned in black, gray, and white, and some, such as the roughtooth and spotted dolphin,

▲ The patches of rough skin on the right whale vary in shape and position. This means that each of these whales can be recognized.

◀ As the humpback whale dives, its huge tail lifts clear of the water, so the pattern on the underside of each fluke can be seen.

DISTRIBUTION

Whales live in seas and oceans all around the world. They live in the cold waters of the Arctic and Antarctic, as well as in warm tropical oceans. The larger whales are animals of the deep oceans, although some follow the line of the coast, especially when traveling long distances. Smaller whales, such as most dolphins, pilot whales, and beaked whales, also swim far out to sea, but humpback dolphins and porpoises are among those that stay in shallow coastal water, harbors, and river estuaries. There are even five species of dolphins that live in freshwater rivers.

As the common dolphin leaps clear of the water, the "hourglass" pattern on its side comes into view. The yellow color may fade in winter.

How Can a Blue Whale Be So Big?

It would not be possible for a land animal to be as large as a blue whale. Its bones would break under its colossal weight. Because water supports the weight of a swimming animal, even a large whale is almost weightless in seawater, so its bones are not overloaded. A whale's bones are actually quite light. Inside each bone is a network of large spaces that are filled with oils and fatty substances that help it float.

I DIDN'T KNOW THAT

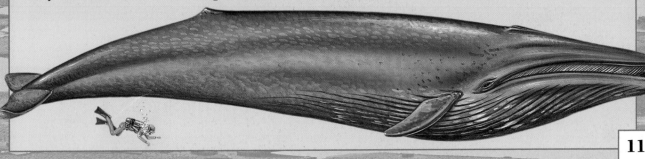

CHAPTER 2
Swimming and Diving

Large baleen whales cruise at speeds from 3 to 12 miles (5 to 20 km) per hour, and some, such as the blue whale, can reach speeds of 30 miles (48 km) per hour for short distance.

A sei whale can reach a speed of 35 miles (about 56 km) per hour for short distances.

Dolphins swimming fast reach a speed of 30 to 35 miles (48 to 56 km) per hour.

Gray whale migration is a tourist attraction in California, where whales can be seen swimming slowly just a short distance offshore.

Whales move by swimming. They are unable to move over land, although some kinds of dolphins can ride waves right to the edge of the shore to catch fish and then wriggle back into deeper water. Whales, dolphins, and porpoises swim by propelling themselves through the water by means of their muscular tail and two broad fins, or flukes.

The upstroke of the tail pushes the whale forward. This is called the power stroke. Then the tail moves downward, so that it is in the right position to make another powerful upstroke. When a whale wants to swim slowly, it makes slow, deep

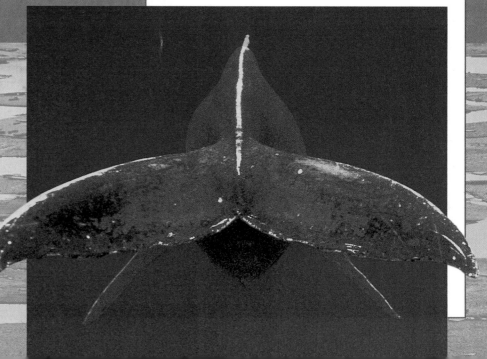

The humpback whale lifts its massive tail to propel itself forward through the water.

strokes with its tail. If it wants to go faster, it makes faster but shallower strokes, beating its tail about twice a second. Its smooth skin and streamlined shape help to reduce friction as it swims through the water.

As the whale glides forward, its flippers help to stabilize it so that the whale does not roll from side to side in the water. Flippers also help a whale to change direction, slow down, and stop.

BOWRIDING

Swimming requires energy, and swimming fast means that even more energy has to be used. Dolphins save energy by using the waves made by the bows of boats and ships as they cut through the water. By positioning its body and tail flukes correctly, dolphins use the energy in the bow wave to move themselves forward

Whales often throw themselves completely clear of the water, landing with a huge splash. This is called breaching. No one knows exactly why whales do this. It could be that they are simply playing!

faster. Species such as bottlenose, striped, and common dolphins often bowride in this way.

13

KEEPING WARM

Like all mammals, whales are warm-blooded. This means their body temperature remains fairly constant. They must be able to keep warm, especially when they are swimming in the cold seas near polar regions. To prevent losing heat to the water, whales have a thick layer of fat, just below the skin, known as blubber. This acts as an insulator, preventing heat from being lost from their blood and muscles. A bowhead whale may have a layer of blubber up to 20 inches (50 centimeters) thick.

If it swims fast for a while, a whale may become too hot. When this happens, it reduces its temperature by increasing the blood flow to its flippers, flukes, and head. In these parts of its body, there is almost no blubber, and so the seawater cools the blood.

I DIDN'T KNOW THAT

Deep Dives

To dive, whales take a series of huge breaths and plunge beneath the surface. Most do not descend far, but sperm whales make incredible dives as deep as 3,000 feet (a little less than 1,000 meters). Large males may stay underwater for up to 2 hours, although most sperm whale dives last about 10 minutes. Sperm whales make almost vertical dives. Recent films have shown that they rest motionless in a vertical position with their heads pointing downward.

ANNUAL MIGRATION

The large baleen whales make long journeys each year. They spend summers in polar waters, feeding on schools of krill, an animal related to shrimp, and small fish. In winter, they travel to warmer waters nearer the equator to mate or give birth. Of the toothed whales, only male sperm

Unlike most other whales, some belugas, such as those that live in the Gulf of St. Lawrence on Canada's eastern seaboard, do not migrate seasonally.

whales make a similar migration. They spend summer feeding on squid in colder waters nearer the polar ice but swim to warmer seas in winter. Females spend all year in warmer water.

CHAPTER 3
Breathing

Whales have to come to the surface to breathe in air. If they cannot do this, they will drown. A whale's nostrils are on the top of its head. This is different from other aquatic mammals, such as seals and sea cows, which have nostrils at the tips of their snouts. A whale's nostrils form a single or double blowhole. Whales close the blowhole while underwater, so that water cannot enter.

When a whale needs to take a breath, it exposes the blowhole above the water and opens it. Stale air is exhaled at great pressure,

This humpback whale, like other baleen whales, has a double blowhole. These are only open when the whale breaks the surface to breathe.

A whale breathes about 2 to 4 times a minute while moving at the surface (people breathe about 15 times per minute).

The air the whale exhales has almost all the oxygen (98 percent) removed from it.

Male sperm whales can stay underwater for over 2 hours, but females stay underwater for only about 40 minutes.

Dolphins dive to depths of about 920 feet (280 m) and can stay underwater for about 8 minutes.

When a baleen whale surfaces to breathe, it makes 10-15 blows, 15 seconds apart.

sending a spume of water vapor plus mucus and oily droplets into the air. This is called a spout or blow. The blow of a large whale is easy to see at a long distance. This is because it rises high into the air, and the water vapor it contains condenses as it meets cooler air.

Whales are able to open their mouths during dives with no fear of drowning because there is no way that water from their mouths can

A humpback whale makes a distinctive "blow." A broad plume of stale air and water vapor spouts about 10 feet (3 m) into the air.

enter their lungs. Most mammals can breathe either through the nose or through the mouth, but a whale can breathe only through its nostrils. The air passages are permanently separated from the gullet down which food passes from the mouth to the stomach. This enables whales to catch and swallow food underwater.

Baleen whales have two nostrils. When they breathe out, a jet of air and water vapor comes from each. In some species these remain distinct, but in others they combine into a single plume. The "blow" of many of these whales is so distinctive that it can be used to identify exactly which kind of whale it is. The blue whale makes a tall, slender plume of spray. A right whale makes two broad spouts of vapor.

Toothed whales have single blowholes. With the notable exception of sperm whales and orcas, toothed whales seldom make a spout large enough to be seen from any distance. The sperm whale is unique among whales because its blowhole is at the tip of its huge head and slightly to the left.

LUNGS

A whale's lungs are very efficient. A whale, dolphin, or porpoise nearly empties its lungs when it breathes out, and almost completely fills them every time it breathes in. This means that almost all of the

The spout from each blowhole of the right whale goes in a different direction, making a characteristic V-shaped blow.

Oxygen Reserves

When a whale dives, it stores virtually all of the oxygen its body needs in its muscles and blood. Oxygen is shifted to the most important organs—the lung, heart, and brain. This explains why a surfacing whale does not suffer from the potentially fatal condition known as "the bends," which is a kind of nitrogen poisoning that affects human divers when they come up too quickly. Essentially, the whale is holding its breath while it dives and resurfaces, which means that the pressure of the water does not force nitrogen into its bloodstream as it breathes. Human divers suffer the bends because they continue to breathe air and oxygen while underwater.

stale air in their lungs is exchanged for fresh air with every breath. By contrast, a person exchanges only about 10 to 20 percent of the amount of air in his or her lungs with every breath. Whales can breathe in and out much faster than people do—a fin whale breathes out all stale air and breathes in fresh air in less than two seconds. Rorquals, which do not dive very deeply, take three or four breaths and are then able to submerge for up to 10 minutes.

CHAPTER 4
Senses and Navigation

A whale's senses enable it to detect and interpret what is happening in its watery world. This is vital to its survival, as it is the means by which it finds food, escapes from danger, or recognizes a possible mate. Whales can see and hear, but underwater, their sense of hearing is more important to them than their eyesight. Sound travels 4.5 times faster in water than it does in air. Light does not travel nearly as well in water as it does in air. Only

The eyes of this gray whale are 6-7 feet (about 2 m) from the top of its snout. In spite of the comparatively small size of their eyes, most whales have good eyesight above water.

Very little daylight penetrates the depths to which sperm whales dive. The only illumination in this darkness comes from sea creatures that can produce their own light.

Although the noise made by a blue whale is the loudest sound produced by any animal—at 188 decibels, louder even than a jet plane—it occurs at too low a frequency to be heard by human ears.

Dolphins can make more than 3,000 clicks per second.

Dolphins are able to locate a tiny fish only three-quarters of an inch (2 cm) long.

Whales do not have a sense of smell, but some toothed whales can taste their food and the water in which they are swimming by means of taste buds on their tongues.

10 percent of the light at the surface reaches depths of just 33 feet (10 meters) of clear water.

These spotted dolphins communicate with each other and work together as a group to round up schools of small fish that they feed on near the surface.

Whales use sound in a number of ways in their daily lives. All whales have a repertoire of whistles, moans, chirps, or thumps that they use to communicate with each other. They have a wide vocabulary, and can let each other know where they are, whether they have found food, if they are hurt or stranded, or if they are looking for a mate. In addition, toothed whales vocalize when they are gathering for a hunt. Toothed whales also produce streams of clicks that they use to navigate and find prey.

SPY-HOPPING

Whales can see both above and below water. Many will stand upright in the water with their heads exposed. In this position they can peer around to inspect fishing boats and other vessels. This habit is known as spy-hopping. The gray whale, the beluga, pilot whales, the orca, and Risso's dolphin are among those species known to spy-hop.

HEARING

Mammals have a pair of inner ears inside their heads that receive sound waves. Sound reaches the inner ear of land animals through openings in the head which are usually surrounded by a large, often furry, outer ear. A whale's ears are arranged differently. There is no external ear, and the opening on the side of the head is tiny and plugged with wax. A whale's inner ears are in cavities filled with a foamy substance.

Exactly how sound travels from the water through a whale's head to its inner ears is not yet known. Scientists think that low sounds may travel along the tube leading from each outer ear opening. They think that higher sounds travel along oily channels in the lower jaw and other bones of toothed whales to reach the inner ears.

When whales such as these orcas want to know what is going on, they can stand upright with the front part of their bodies right out of the water. They need to turn their whole body around to look in all directions.

MAKING A NOISE

Whales communicate with each other by making an amazing variety of noises. Some of these are outside the range of human hearing, but others are clearly audible. In the past, whalers could identify some whales from the sound they made.

The very low sounds made by baleen whales travel enormous distances through the water. Communicating by means of such sounds is the way in which individual baleen whales keep in contact with others of their own kind.

Sailors called the beluga "the sea canary" because its melodious underwater "chatter" could be heard clearly aboard ship.

SONG OF THE WHALE

In 1970, a California record company produced a most unusual record. It was a recording of the sequence of sounds made by a male humpback whale. The "songs" of the male humpback are made up of many different sequences of sounds, so that each song may last 6 to 30 minutes. Male humpbacks have been known to sing one song after another for up to 24 hours. These songs can be heard by other humpbacks as far as 20 miles (32 km) away.

By means of echolocation, a toothed whale can scan the underwater environment, even in complete darkness, to locate and avoid obstacles, to find schools of fish, and to pinpoint the exact location of one fish or squid.

ECHOLOCATION

Toothed whales have an inbuilt sonar system that helps them to navigate and to find food. This system is called echolocation. This is how it works. When sound waves hit an object, an echo bounces back. We can hear echoes of our voices if we shout in a cave or steep-sided valley. Dolphins and other toothed whales can emit a steady stream of clicking sounds that pass out through a fatty lump called a melon, near the back of the upper jaw. The melon focuses the stream of clicks into a beam.

The sound waves hit underwater objects such as rocks, wrecks, nets, and fish, producing another stream of rebounding echoes. This is picked up by and passes through the toothed whale's lower jaw and into its inner ear. The hearing of these whales is extremely sensitive to these echoes. They can distinguish between objects and know where they are from the kind of echoes that they hear.

I DIDN'T KNOW THAT

River Dolphins

There are five species of river dolphins. They live in the major rivers of South America (the Amazon and the Orinoco); India, Pakistan, and Bangladesh (the Indus and the Ganges); and China (the Yangtze). All five species are very rare, and all five have very poor eyesight.

CHAPTER 5
Food and Feeding

All whales, from the largest baleen whales to the smallest porpoises, are predators that need to catch living prey. How they do this, and what kinds of prey they catch, varies from species to species. The largest baleen whales eat some of the smallest animals! Baleen whales are filter feeders. They filter, or strain, small fish and other tiny animals swimming near the surface of the sea by passing large quantities of water through their bristly plates of baleen.

The toothed whales are more active hunters, often working in groups to round up a school of fish and then taking turns to catch their fill.

This bottlenose dolphin will soon catch and eat any fish that are not quite as fit as the rest.

A blue whale's mouth holds up to 18,000 gallons (about 70,000 liters) of water.

Sei whales, which can measure up to 50 feet (15 m) long, filter out and eat tiny living organisms less than a half inch (1.25 cm) long.

A blue whale eats an estimated 40 million krill (a shrimp-like animal) every day. That's four tons of krill daily.

An adult sperm whale eats a ton of food a day.

The orca regularly catches the largest prey of all whales—sea lions, manta rays, and seals.

They may have to chase their prey fast in order to catch it. The teeth of most toothed whales are sharp and pointed to catch and hold onto slippery fish and squid, but these teeth cannot cut up or grind food, so almost all of these whales swallow their prey whole. Porpoises are an exception. They have chisel-shaped teeth that are able to cut chunks off the larger fish that they catch on the bed of shallow coastal waters.

FILTER FEEDERS

When a baleen whale feeds, it takes in a mouthful of water, together with all the plankton (small fish and other tiny animals) that it contains. As it closes its mouth, the whale's huge tongue pushes up, forcing the water out of the sides of the mouth through the baleen plates. The fringed edges of the baleen plates form a mat of fibers on each side of the mouth. When the mouth is completely shut, the whale swallows its catch.

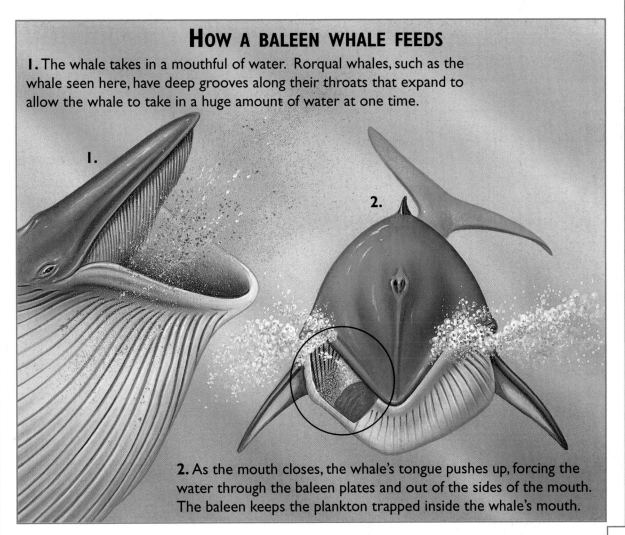

HOW A BALEEN WHALE FEEDS

1. The whale takes in a mouthful of water. Rorqual whales, such as the whale seen here, have deep grooves along their throats that expand to allow the whale to take in a huge amount of water at one time.

2. As the mouth closes, the whale's tongue pushes up, forcing the water through the baleen plates and out of the sides of the mouth. The baleen keeps the plankton trapped inside the whale's mouth.

Rorquals are six types of baleen whales, such as this humpback, that have grooves along their throats. These grooves allow the whale to open its mouth enormously wide when it feeds.

Baleen whales do not all filter out food in exactly the same way. The gray whale stirs up the sediment on the seabed with its snout. Then it takes a mouthful of the sandy or muddy water and filters out all the small animals it has dislodged through rows of short, stiff plates of baleen. Right and bowhead whales have deep lower lips that curve up, hiding very long baleen plates. These whales swim along slowly with their mouths open, straining plankton from the water as it passes through the two curtains of baleen.

EXPERT HUNTERS

The orca, known also as the killer whale, is the only whale that eats warm-blooded prey such as seals, dolphins, and penguins. Orcas also eat squid, bony fish, and sharks. A group of five to ten orcas in polar regions may spy-hop to see if there is a seal sitting on a small ice-floe. When they find one, they all swim toward the floe together, turning sideways as they approach. This sends a large wave over the ice, washing the seal into the water, and into the waiting jaws of another orca. Although orcas cannot slice chunks off their prey with their pointed teeth, they can tear it apart by repeatedly tossing it into the air.

On the Menu

The sperm whale feeds mostly on squid that it catches at depths from a few feet down to 3,000 feet (over 900 meters). These large whales also eat a variety of other slow-moving prey, including bottom-feeding sharks, skates, jellyfish, and angler fish. Other more unexpected items have also been found inside their stomachs, including coconuts, boots, and even a bucket!

I DIDN'T KNOW THAT

CHAPTER 6
Reproduction

There is still a lot that we do not know about how some kinds of whales choose their mates. Even the biggest of them all, the blue whale, has kept its courting behavior a secret from us. Little also is known about the courtship of beaked whales. Others have not been so shy. Males and females of the great right whale start their energetic courtship by repeatedly leaping out of the water and breaching. Humpbacks chase each

Courting humpback whales are very boisterous, chasing each other through the water and making loud splashes with their tails.

Gestation, which is the length of time it takes for a whale to develop inside its mother before birth, lasts from 8 to 16 months, depending on the species.

A newborn blue whale can be up to 27 feet (7.8 m) long and usually weighs about 3 tons.

A mother blue whale produces about 50 gallons (200 l) of milk a day for her offspring.

A blue whale calf gains about 200 pounds (90 kg) a day for the first week of its life.

other, making splashes with their tails. Longfin pilot whales head-butt each other. By contrast, bottlenose dolphins swim close together, touching each other with their flippers. Some scientists believe that the songs of male humpback whales are used to attract females.

Male whales compete with each other in order to win mates. When it is time for sperm whales to mate, the males travel to the females, which live together in small groups in warm seas toward the equator. The largest males battle fiercely. They charge each

Male narwhals fight with their long, sharp tusks. Injuries are common, and tusks often get broken.

other head-on. They grip each other's lower jaws and wrestle, often breaking teeth or even the lower jaw itself in the process.

Male narwhals fence with their long, spirally twisted tusks. A tusk can grow to 10 feet (3 meters) in length. These trials of strength may be little more than show, but male narwhals sometimes carry the scars from these battles for the rest of their life. Beaked whale males also fight fiercely, slashing at each other with their teeth.

BIRTH

Whales and dolphins either mate at the surface or just below the water. After mating, the young whale develops inside its mother's body for many months until it is ready to be born. Blue whale calves are often born tailfirst, while orcas are often born headfirst. As soon as it is born, the female helps her calf to the surface so it can breathe. Like

A humpback calf feeds from its mother for its first year of life. During this time, the calf stays close to its mother for protection.

other mammals, female whales feed their young from their own body, providing a rich, fatty milk.

A NEW LIFE

When it has taken its first breath, and had its first meal, a new born whale is able to follow its mother.

The calf has to feed underwater between breaths. The milk is pumped from the mother's body to help the calf to feed and the young calf grows quickly.

GROWING UP

By the time it is half-grown, the calf no longer needs to feed from its mother, but it may stay with her for longer. Young calves are very playful, nipping their mother's tail flukes and wriggling over her back. Mothers guard their calves if a predator threatens, and a gray whale mother may even lift a young calf out of danger with a flipper.

Life is fun for a young dolphin, but it is hard work as well. The calf has to learn how to catch its own fish and to recognize and avoid danger.

Although small whales, such as porpoises or dolphins, may start breeding at a young age (3-5 years old for females, 6 to 8 years old for males), this does not mean they are fully grown. It takes many years for a large whale to reach its full size. A male great sperm whale is not full-grown until it is 35 years old. Porpoises may live for up to 23 years, some dolphins up to 50 years, and some of the larger whales live even longer than that. A sperm whale can live for 70 years, while a humpback generally lives to 40 or so. It is believed that some fin whales can live to be 100.

A FAMILY GROUP

Northern bottlenose whales are among those that live all year in a family group of about one to four whales. Each group contains one adult male and a small number of females and their calves. Orcas live in family groups of five to twenty. One-fifth of these are adult males, but there is only one dominant male. He is easy to spot because he has the longest dorsal fin.

In this group of orcas, five males, with tall, upright dorsal fins, can be seen. The shorter, more curved fin of a female orca can be seen on the whale to the far right.

Slow Breeders

Whales reproduce slowly. Female whales of many species may produce only one calf every three or four years. Even porpoises only have one calf every two years. This means that a female bottlenose dolphin with a life of about 35 years will give birth to just eight calves.

CHAPTER 7
Social Skills

A group of whales is known as a pod.

Unlike most baleen whales, fin whales live in groups, which number from 3 to 20 animals.

A school of common dolphins may consist of hundreds of dolphins.

Most whales are social animals that seem to enjoy the presence of other whales, whether they live close to each other all year or migrate great distances. Marine biologists have learned that the way whales communicate with each other is very complex. Studying animals in their natural environment is the best way of learning about them, but in the case of whales, which spend all their time roaming the oceans, this can be very difficult.

Many kinds of dolphins, including orcas, can be kept in captivity in aquariums and marine parks. Although many people think that it is unkind to keep dolphins in captivity it has enabled scientists to study them more easily than in the wild. Much has been learned about dolphin intelligence and echolocation as a result of such study. Dolphins and orcas in captivity fascinate all who go to see them. They are quick to learn tricks, and to copy the activities of other mammals, including humans.

This orca is performing its routine at a Seaworld Center in California.

COOPERATION

Dolphins and other whales that live in groups cooperate to perform many tasks. They work together during a hunt, rounding up schools of fish. Females often help each other during birth. Some have been seen gently tugging on the tail flukes of a baby to speed up a birth. Once the calf is born, a number of females help the mother to nudge the calf to the surface so it can breathe. Dolphins often work together to communicate the presence of predators to each other.

A group of humpbacks blows a "net" of bubbles to drive a school of fish close together. Then they lunge up to the surface with their mouths open, each whale scooping up many fish.

CARE OF THE SICK

A whale that cannot reach the surface of the water will drown. Dolphins and other whales quickly detect signs of distress in their own and other species. They push the injured animal to the surface so it can breathe. There are even tales of dolphins coming to the aid of a drowning person. The larger whales also respond to distress signals of others of their own kind. If one is injured, others surround it to protect it from attack by other predators.

I DIDN'T KNOW THAT

Friendly Dolphins

The friendly nature of bottlenose dolphins delights many people who go to see them in aquariums. Children are able to feed some of them fish from their hands, as well as watch them performing stunts such as leaping through hoops suspended above the water. Occasionally, wild dolphins seek out people bathing in the sea and appear to enjoy their company. Along parts of the southwest coast of Great Britain in the mid-1970s, a male bottlenose dolphin called Beaky became famous for coming close to shore to play with swimmers.

STRANDING

Occasionally either single whales or groups of whales swim onto shore, where they are stranded. Exactly why this happens is unknown. Sometimes it may be caused by disease or injury. If a sick whale becomes stranded, the other members of its group may try so hard to help it that they too become stranded. But often what appear to be perfectly healthy

This sperm whale is one of six that was stranded on a beach in northeast Scotland. All six died.

whales become stranded. It can be difficult to save stranded whales. Their weight makes all but the smallest difficult to move. Exposed to the air, their skin dries and cracks. Sadly, stranded whales that are rescued often soon strand themselves again.

CHAPTER 8
Threats and Conservation

Without doubt, the greatest threat to whales has been from the whaling industry. Whales are a good source of meat and oil. People have hunted whales for centuries, but they did not threaten the survival of whales as species until the last half of the 19th century. More efficient ways of killing whales were invented at this time, and these led to the establishment of whaling stations and factory ships in the Antarctic and other parts of the world during the first half of the 20th century.

This fin whale is being cut up and processed in a whaling station in southwest Iceland.

 In the Antarctic summer of 1930-31, 30,000 blue whales were killed by whalers.

 In the traditional whale hunt held in the Faroe Islands, a school of pilot whales is driven ashore and killed.

Until vegetable substitutes became available, whale oil was used to make margarine.

 Gill nets set by Japanese fishermen to catch salmon may cause the death by drowning of over 10,000 Dall's porpoises every year.

Environmental Pollution

Coastal dolphins and porpoises are threatened by pollution that either originates on land, or is caused by ships discharging pollutants at sea. The belugas that live in the Gulf of St. Lawrence in Canada have high levels of poisonous chemicals in their bodies. Many of these have come from prey such as eels that have traveled from lakes polluted with industrial waste to the estuary, where they are eaten by the whales.

At its height, the whaling industry killed tens of thousands of the large baleen whales every year. Blue, gray, and right whales were caught in such large numbers that these species were in danger of dying out. Now they are protected, but their populations have still not recovered from the heavy losses caused by the whaling industry.

Some smaller whales are now endangered by habitat changes, pollution, and over-fishing by rural communities. The Indus river dolphin and the Gulf porpoise are under threat because irrigation schemes affecting the Indus and Colorado rivers have destroyed their natural habitat. Today, many organizations work to protect all species of whales.

TRADITIONAL WHALE HUNTERS

In places such as the Faroe Islands, Siberia, Alaska, and the Caribbean islands of St. Vincent and the Grenadines, whale hunting is a part of the traditional culture. Today, these communities do not necessarily need whale products for their survival or a successful economy. Many people feel that killing any whale is cruel and unnecessary. However, the inhabitants of these places consider whaling to be an important part of their way of life.

OTHER THREATS

Dolphins and porpoises can become entangled in fishing nets and lines that are not intended to harm them. Unable to reach the surface to breathe, such trapped

This is the aftermath of a "traditional" pilot whale hunt in the Faroe Islands. The Faroese consider the hunt an important part of their culture. Others think it should be banned.

animals drown before the nets are brought to the surface. "Dolphin-friendly" fishing gear helps to reduce instances of this happening, but dolphins and porpoises are still the unintentional victims of squid and tuna fishing.

INTERNATIONAL WHALING COMMISSION

The International Whaling Commission was created in 1946 in order to regulate the whaling industry. At first, the Commission was more concerned with ensuring the secure future of the industry. By the 1970s, the conservation of whales had become an important issue, but it was not until 1982 that the Commission agreed to a moratorium (a temporary suspension) on all commercial whaling. This finally came into effect in 1986, although a few countries such as Japan were permitted to catch quotas of whales such as minkes for scientific purposes.

WHALE CONSERVATION

The Whale and Dolphin Conservation Society, Save the Whales, and Greenpeace are just three of the many organizations that work to see that no species of whale become extinct. Such work is called conservation. These organizations raise public awareness of issues that threaten whales. In the case of Greenpeace, they sometimes use controversial methods to stop whale hunting. We owe it to future generations to do all that they can to prevent any species of whale from becoming extinct.

Television documentaries and conservation organizations have done much to raise public awareness about threats to the future survival of whales, but some nations, such as Japan, continue to hunt whales.

Glossary

BALEEN WHALE – Type of whale that has horny plates, called baleen, hanging from each side of the upper jaw instead of teeth. Each plate of baleen has a fringe of fibers down one side and is used to strain food from seawater

BLOWHOLE – The nostril or nostrils at the top of a whale's head through which the animal breathes

BLUBBER – The thick layer of fat under a whale's skin that covers most of its body except its head, flippers, and flukes

BREACHING – When a whale throws itself completely clear of the water, then lands with a huge splash

CALF – A young whale

CARNIVORE – An animal that eats flesh

DORSAL FIN – The single fin found on the back of most whales

ECHOLOCATION – The way in which a toothed whale uses sound to navigate and find food in dark water.

EXTINCT – When no more animals of a species remain alive

FLUKES – The pair of broad, horizontal fins on the whale's tail that it uses to propel itself through the water

INSULATOR – A substance that does not allow heat to pass easily through it. In whales, blubber acts as an insulator.
KERATIN – A type of protein from which baleen is made

MIGRATION – The seasonal movement of animals from one area to another

PLANKTON – Small fish and other tiny animals that drift in oceans, lakes, and rivers

POD – A group of orcas (killer whales)

POLLUTION – Contamination of the environment with substances that are harmful to life

PREDATOR – An animal that hunts another animal for food

PREY – An animal that is caught and eaten by another animal

SPECIES – A kind or type of animal

SPY-HOPPING – Type of behavior by some whales in which they stand upright in the water, with their heads exposed, in order to look around

STRANDING – When a whale or group of whales swims onto or near shore and cannot get back to deep water

TOOTHED WHALES – The group of whales, including dolphins and porpoises, that have teeth rather than plates of baleen

VOCALIZE – To form a sound

WARM-BLOODED – Animals such as mammals that are able to maintain a fairly constant body temperature

Further Reading

Carwardine, Mark. *Whales, Dolphins, and Porpoises*. New York: DK, 1992.

Frahm, Randy. *The Humpback Whale*. Danbury, CT: Children's Press, 1997.

Oakley, Mark. *Whales and Dolphins*. New York: Penguin, 1992.

Petty, Kate. *Whales Can Sing: And Other Amazing Facts About Sea Mammals*. Brookfield, CT: Millbrook, 1998.

Simon, Seymour. *Whales*. New York: Harper Collins, 1992.

Organizations to Contact

American Cetacean Society
P.O. Box 1391
San Pedro, CA 90733-1391
www.acsonline.org

The Dolphin Institute
1129 Ala Moana Boulevard
Honolulu, HI 96814
(808) 593-2211
www.dolphin-institute.com

Whale and Dolphin Conservation Society
Alexander House
James Street West
Bath BA1 2BT
UK
www.wdcs.org

World Wildlife Fund
1250 Twenty-Fourth Street, N.W.
P.O. Box 97180
Washington, DC 20077-7180
www.worldwildlife.org

Acknowledgments
Cover: Bruce Coleman Collection; p.8: Gerard Soury/Oxford Scientific Films; p.9: Bruce Coleman Collection; p.10: Pacific Stock/Bruce Coleman Collection; p.11: Mark Carwardine/Bruce Coleman Collection; p.12: Pacific Stock/Bruce Coleman Collection; p.13: Pacific Stock/Bruce Coleman Collection; p.14: Howard Hall/Oxford Scientific Films; p.15: Gunter Ziesler/Bruce Coleman Collection; p.16: Mark Carwardine/Bruce Coleman Collection; p.17: Daniel J.Cox/Oxford Scientific Films; p.18: Haroldo Palo Jr./Natural History Photographic Agency; p.19: Bill Wood/Bruce Coleman Collection; p.20: Norbert Wu/Natural History Photographic Agency; p.21: Mark Carwardine/Bruce Coleman Collection; page 22: Kim Westerkov/Oxford Scientific Films; p.23: Doug Allan/Oxford Scientific Films; p.25: Mark Carwardine/Bruce Coleman Collection; p.26: Norbert Wu/Oxford Scientific Films; p.28: A.N.T./Natural History Photographic Agency; p.29: Howard Hall/Oxford Scientific Films; p.30: Pacific Stock/Bruce Coleman Collection; p.31:Doug Allan/Oxford Scientific Films; p. 32: Pacific Stock/Bruce Coleman Collection; p.33: E.Bjurstrom/Bruce Coleman Collection; p.34: Bruce Coleman Collection; p.35: Tui de Roy/Oxford Scientific Films; p.36: Daniel Heuclin/Natural History Photographic Agency; p.37: David E.Myers/Natural History Photographic Agency; p.38: Pacific Stock/Bruce Coleman Collection; p.39: Trevor McDonald/Natural History Photographic Agency; p.40: Mark Carwardine/Bruce Coleman Collection; p.41: Pacific Stock/Bruce Coleman Collection; p.42: Tony Martin/Oxford Scientific Films; p.43: Jeff Foott/Bruce Coleman Collection.

Index

Numbers in *italic* indicate pictures